D1337383

ACC. NO. BK48987

CLASS NO. 746.092/C

MID CHESHIRE COLLEGE

ORDER NO. C94779

This book is to be returned on or before
the last date stamped below.

BK48987

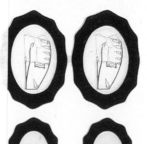
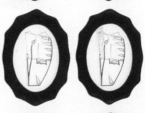

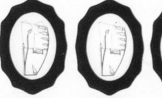
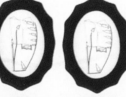

Authors: Elissa Auther, Adam Lerner &
Debra Rubino
Editor: Matthew Koumis
Graphic Design: Rachael Dadd & MK
Photography: Dan Meyers
Reprographics: Ermanno Beverari
Printed in Italy by Grafiche AZ, Verona

© Telos Art Publishing 2003

Telos Limited
PO Box 125, Winchester
SO23 7UJ England
T   +44 (0) 1962 864546
F   +44 (0) 1962 864727
E   editorial@telos.net
E   sales@telos.net
W www.telos.net

ISBN 1 902015 79 7 (softback)
ISBN 1 902015 80 0 (hardback)

A CIP catalogue record for this book is
available from The British Library

The rights of Annet Couwenberg,
Elissa Auther, Adam Lerner & Debra
Rubino to be identified as the author
of their work has been asserted by
them in accordance with the
Copyright, Designs and Patents Act
1988. All rights reserved. No part of
this publication may be reproduced,
stored in a retrieval system or
transmitted in any form or by any
means, without the prior permission in
writing of the publishers.
Photocopying this book is illegal.

Notes

All dimensions are shown in metric
and imperial, height x width x depth.

Artist's Acknowledgments

This book was made possible with the
generous help of many people.
I would like to thank all my studio
assistants: Cynthia Eguez-Estlund,
Gina Denton, Jeanne Hoel, Melanie
Lester, Lesley McTague, Tara Pelletier
and Melissa Rudder for their
committed work ethic, attention to
detail and entertaining stories.
Also thanks to O.L.Horton for his
inspirational drawings. Many thanks to
my supportive colleagues and friends
at the Maryland Institute College of
Art. A special thanks to Elissa Auther
and Adam Lerner, Debra Rubino,
Laura Burns for their excellent writing
and considered thoughts. Your
illuminating insights are appreciated.

Last but not least my gratitude goes
out to my husband and daughter, Dan
and Mara Meyers. You both offered
personalized versions of unconditional
support, inspirational ideas, patience
and tough critiques.

This book is dedicated to my mother
and daughter with love.

Publisher's Acknowledgments

Thanks to Paul Richardson, Simone,
Sue Atkinson, Dennis, Susan, Kasia,
Ermanno, Stefania, Giuseppe.

Photo Captions

page 1:
Precious View
2002
digitized embroidery, fabric,
flocked frame
90 x 95 x 1in
(234 x 247 x 2.6cm)

page 4:
Flat Collar #1
2000
flock, masonite, steel T-pins
42 x 84in
(109 x 216cm)

page 6:
Embroidery Frolic #2
2000
digitized embroidery, fabric, pins,
flock, shadowbox
21 x 17 x 1.5in
(55 x 44 x 4cm)

page 48:
**Act Normal and That's Crazy
Enough**
(detail)
2002
starched cotton, reed, copper wire,
computer embroidery, fabric

portfolio collection
Annet Couwenberg

TELOS

Contents

Foreword

"Art is among the experiences I rely on to alter what I am."

'The Object Stares Back'
James Elkins

The work of an exquisite, elegant hand is always evident in the fiber constructions made by Annet Couwenberg. As a whole, her pieces speak in a contemporary voice, even while a deeply embedded classicism is the underscore. The body of work she has created over the last 20 years involves a higher level of complexity with each piece she makes; yet, it is always accessible, and often, frolicsome.

Fourteen years ago I met Annet Couwenberg when she arrived in Baltimore, Maryland, to become chair of the fiber department at the Maryland Institute College of Art.

In the years since, she has built the department into one of the best in the country, in large measure because of her unflagging commitment to her students and because of her incredible energy and intelligence. She is at once an artist, a teacher, mother, wife, daughter, sister, and a friend – and while she is engaged with equal dedication to them all individually, all of those roles are also critical to her work.

Growing up in the Netherlands as a young girl, she watched her mother, grandmother, and aunts as they gathered together in weekly sessions filled with fabric and mending, needles and pins, thread and stitching. She recognized later in her career, that the clothing was not what most engaged her imagination; rather, it was the women collected together to share of themselves. For them this setting provided a means of expression and self-definition.

As the small child in the corner, Annet observed them all, fascinated, silent, and largely ignored as they went about their task. "But there is no such thing as just looking," notes James Elkins, in his book, 'The Object Stares Back'. She later came to realize that her childhood voyeurism would translate into something much larger. Clothing, she understood, was a rich repository for these women; the habitual gathering reflected many different aspects of their lives. The construction, the 'making' of the clothing wasn't the focal point of her mind's eye, but rather, she questioned how clothes functioned as an exterior representative of the interior. The weekly gatherings were, for her, multi-layered. They were at once a political indication of social standing, a reflection of personality and character that could be readily apparent or deeply mysterious, while the clothing provided clues, connecting women in their own personal search for identity.

As an outside observer, even at that early age, she cherished the role of investigator. For her, apparel became a way to construct and deconstruct identity and she felt drawn to understand the underlying structure not only in its physical form, but metaphorically. How clothing relates to the body and its metaphorical underpinnings became a fascination, a personal obsession. It is not surprising that in her work, the focus is an unrelenting dialogue about the internal structure versus the façade.

Annet Couwenberg's work has been described in many different ways, perhaps because what makes it most compelling is that it defies definition. She has been called a fiber artist, a sculptor, and a feminist. But she considers herself to be more of a builder, an engineer committed to "sublime order." She works with humble materials – copper mesh, flocking, starched linen, thread, wood and feathers – chosen because they represent the utilitarian, a trait inherited from her Dutch upbringing.

In her work, a viewer sees the obsessive attention to detail and repetition – again, a work ethic forever inculcated into her personality. But she left the Netherlands 20 years ago – although she still feels strongly connected to her Dutch heritage – to be able to expand upon her own tradition and to celebrate a more untethered approach to her work. Here, in the United States, she has embraced multiple approaches to an art form that allows her pieces to be incredibly expansive. As a teacher, she is committed to bringing new methodologies to her students; thus, she has become a student, herself – originally to understand and share the techniques – of wood-working, sculpture, digitized embroidery, and 3-D Studio. Inevitably, what she learns as a committed teacher finds its way into her new pieces, making them even more complex and provocative.

She fabricates new works and incorporates new methodologies, but the final piece always embraces the textile tradition.

When you look at the pieces in this book, you will see a rich array that represents an on-going artistic and intellectual exploration by Annet Couwenberg. She possesses a complex, idiosyncratic vision, an insistent curiosity and fascination with the body, its armature, and commonplace materials which, altogether once caught in her hands, transcend in a breath-taking ascendance.

Debra Rubino
Artist & writer

right:
Embroidery Frolic #3
2000
digitized embroidery, fabric, pins, flock, shadowbox
21 x 17 x 1.5in (55 x 44 x 4cm)

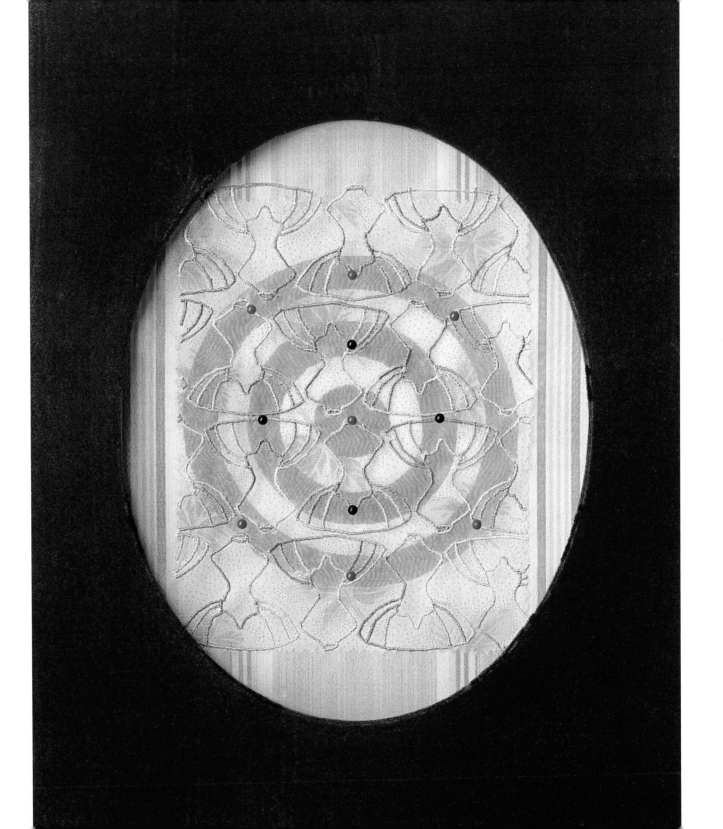

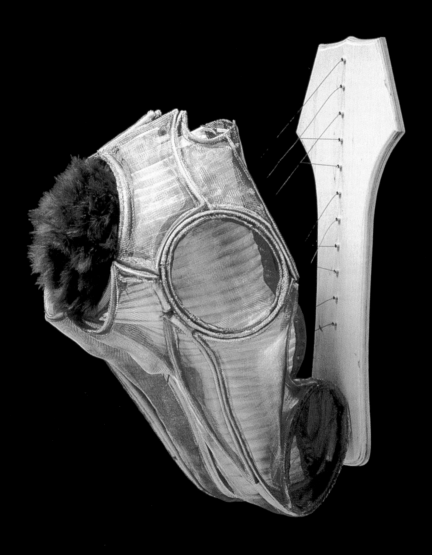

The Tailor Retailoring

left:

Untitled #3
1996
copper screen, pleated silk, reed,
feathers, wood, cable
30 x 24 x 16in (78 x 62 x 41cm)

"Neither in tailoring nor in legislating does man proceed by mere Accident... In all his Modes and... endeavours an Architectural Idea will be found lurking; his Body and the Cloth are the site and materials whereon and whereby his beautiful edifice, of a Person, is to be built."

Thomas Carlyle,
'Sartor Resartus,' 1833
[The Tailor Retailored]

opposite:
B.U.G. (Body Under Garment)
1989
copper screen, reed,
wire, wood, feathers
60 x 28 x 26in (156 x 73 x 68cm)

Annet Couwenberg's recent sculpture, *Act Normal* (2002), a group of stacked, ruffled forms resembling Dutch collars, exemplifies an aesthetic impulse that has been central to her work for the past twenty years. Recognizable to art lovers from likenesses in so many seventeenth-century Dutch paintings, the collars are constructed of starched white cotton held taught by reed armatures. Couwenberg is known for the kind of meticulous, labor-intensive, handwork that produces the striking visual effect of this sculpture. However, it is not merely the materials and processes that lend Couwenberg's work their enormous force. The size of these objects moves them beyond clothing and approximates the scale of furniture. The notion of clothing as a structure to contain the human body, like furniture or architecture, lies at the core of Couwenberg's aesthetic drive.

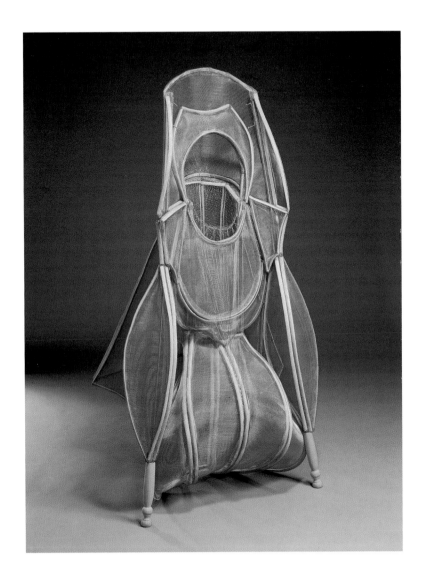

Clothing, Structure, Architecture

Couwenberg's interest in the relationship of clothing to architecture began early in her career when she was asked to design fabrics incorporating complicated systems of pleats for New York fashion designer Ronald Kolodzie in the early 1980s. This work afforded her the opportunity to explore textiles as structures, an issue she had begun to consider in a series of relief sculptures incorporating pleated, hand-dyed fabric exhibited a year earlier. It is typical of Couwenberg's penetrating ability to see underlying forms that she would draw a connection between pleats and architecture: they both consist of three-dimensional space created with two-dimensional materials.

Soon after Couwenberg established the relationship between dressmaking and architecture, she began to breathe life into it by introducing the body. This triangulation can be seen in works such as *Seeing is Forgetting the Thing One Sees* (1987) or *B.U.G. (Body Under Garment)* (1989). Both works are composed of wooden armatures that allude to the human torso over which has been stretched copper screen. They also incorporate found architectural or furniture elements. Couwenberg has explained that this series of works was inspired by the highly angular dress patterns of the Anglo-American fashion designer Charles James active between the 1930s and 50s. The influence of his designs, which were the first to exploit the bias of the fabric for architectonic effect, can be seen in these works in the clear delineation of interlocking or fitted shapes that compose their skeletons. The incorporation of what could be a portion of a balustrade in *Seeing is Forgetting*. . . and chair legs in *B.U.G.* emphasizes clothing's connection to larger structures of the built world as containers for the body.

Couwenberg's work manifests the equation articulated by artist-cum-architect Vito Acconci: "furniture is midway between clothing and architecture." According to Acconci, "the way the skin covers the bones, clothing contains the body: a chair then, contains the body-contained-by-clothing – a room then contains the body-contained-by-clothing-contained-by-chair." While clothing is mobile and conforming, and architecture stabile and rigid, furniture lies between the two, somewhat mobile, though fairly rigid. The powerful ambiguity in works like *B.U.G.* and *Seeing is Forgetting* is precisely the ambiguity between body, clothing, furniture and architecture. Their structural autonomy and verticality relate them to furniture and architecture, but the fact that they consist around an armature relates them to clothing and the body. Couwenberg shares with Acconci an interest in the way bodies relate to the forms that contain them. His *Adjustable Wall Bra* is an article of clothing, which is normally used for bodily support, enlarged and transformed so that is becomes at once a piece of furniture to give the body rest and an architectural space to enclose the body. The major difference between Acconci's furniture series and this series of works by Couwenberg is that Acconci's work functions literally as furniture and architecture for actual human bodies, while Couwenberg invokes furniture, architecture and bodies metaphorically.

Couwenberg's use of the body metaphor is a powerful aspect of her work. In pieces such as *Slip Over Pinch* (1996) and *Biased Point* (1996), the association with the human body is especially strong. The 'skeletal' structure, thin copper screen and silk that forms the 'skin' of these works serve as metaphors for the human skeleton and skin. The redness of the copper gives it a particularly anatomic appearance. But, as Acconci points out, all clothing is a kind of skin. Therefore, Couwenberg's work reminds us that all clothing is a metaphor for the body. Seeing truly is forgetting the thing one sees because

when we look at her sculpture we see a body and we forget we could just as well see it as clothing. The haunting quality of her work derives from the way she binds the relationship between clothing and body so tightly we can't distinguish between the clothing and the body on which it rests.

Couwenberg finds deep meaning in the simple fact that clothing on display requires some kind of support. Whereas in fashion shows, actual human bodies provide such support, in department stores, mannequins or hangers support clothing by simulating the human body. Couwenberg's sculptures support their clothing/skin with an armature that similarly acts as a surrogate for the body. This structure is not subservient to the skin as a hanger is clearly subservient to the dress that hangs upon it. Importantly, the skin is also not subservient to the structure, as clothing can be said to decorate the body. This parity between body and ornament can itself be seen as a metaphor for the leveling of the hierarchy between fine and

decorative art that her work enacts. Her works are as much figurative sculptures as they are textiles supported in imaginative forms.

The structural support in Couwenberg's work not only relates it to the body but also to the tradition of sculpture. The work of Beverly Semmes provides a fruitful contrast. Semmes is known for her oversized dresses and robes, where richly colored fabrics cascade down walls and create pools of color on the floor. Semmes exploits fabric insofar as it approximates a liquid, associating her work most closely with painting. Couwenberg, on the other hand, uses fabric for its capacity to act as a membrane to define volumes of space. Her work, therefore, belongs more essentially to a tradition of sculpture. Given the uncanny nature of her forms, combined with the tactility of her materials, Couwenberg's work bears a strong resemblance to Surrealist sculpture wherein the function of materials is to provoke a physical response through its association with touch.

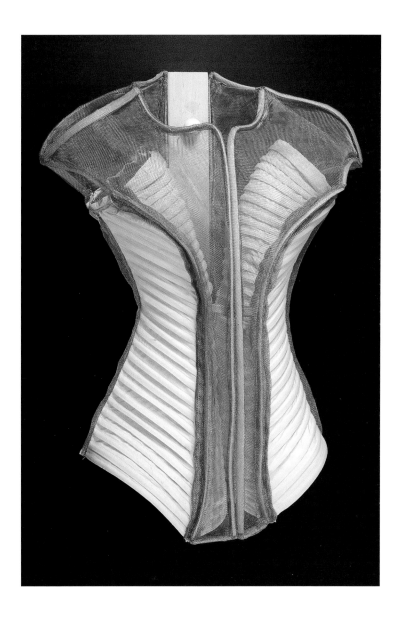

Tailoring the Body

The essential connection between body and dress in Couwenberg's work is the foundation of its social content as seen in her works of the early to mid-1990s dominated by girdle and corset-like forms that squeeze, shape, or sheath the body. In these works, distortions in the clothing design are indistinguishable from deformations of the body. The body is not a given upon which the ornament of clothing is added. These forms of clothing were made to tailor the body, not the other way around. The artist's installation of these works in 1995 was suitably titled *Public Apparel / Private Structures* for the way in which women's undergarments function as a weigh station of sorts between the private body and one's public appearance fashioned in accordance with patriarchal norms of beauty.

left:

Slip over Pinch

1996

pleated silk, copper screen,

reed, wire, wood

28 x 23 x 10in (73 x 60 x 26cm)

right:

Biased Point

1996

pleated silk, copper screen,

reed, wire, wood

36 x 19 x 13in (94 x 49 x 34cm)

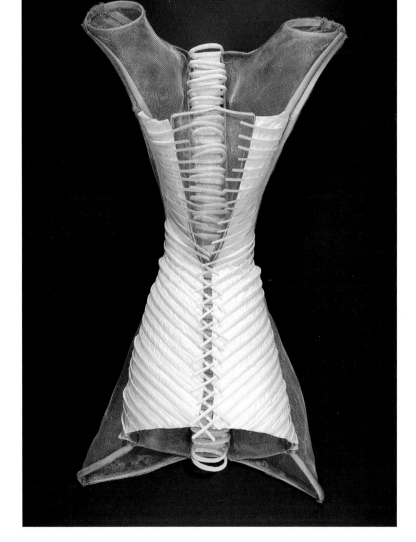

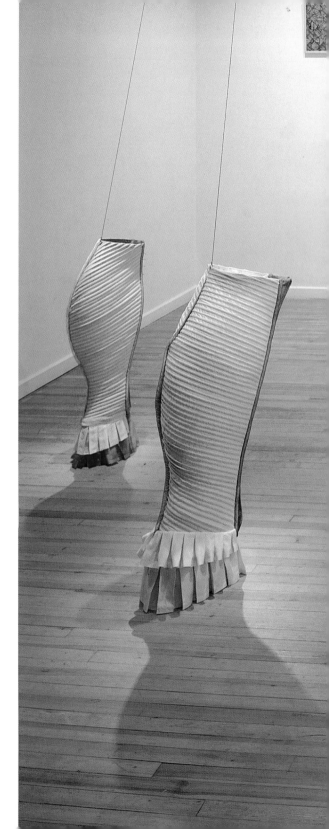

The installation is composed of five, free-standing, body girdles based upon the Victorian bustle. Each girdle's shell is composed of pleated white silk that serves as a container for various interior treatments of folds and wood ribbing or materials such as wire and feathers. On the wall opposite the girdles is a group of stitched abstractions, palimpsests really, composed of layers of dressmaking patterns, rubbings, and machine stitching. Couwenberg connects the three dimensional girdles with the two dimensional abstractions through a series of cables that terminate in the middle of the central stitched abstraction.

Public Apparel/ Private Structures
1995
pleated silk, reed, wire,
copper screen, cables
wall pieces: seminole patchwork,
dressmaking patterns, feathers,
metal screw
9 x 5 x 11in (23 x 13 x 29cm)

Public Apparel / Private Structures plays upon the relationship between fine art and fashion, with the wall abstractions suggestive of the former and the girdles of the latter. The cable that connects one component to the other and mutually supports them can be read as a metaphor for the more general affinity between these forms. The installation as a whole seems to offer a gloomy vision of Victorian propriety and taste. It suggests that the norms that govern women's fashion belong inescapably to the same world in which fine art works are displayed. Tying fine art with fashion, the cable ties eternal forms to fleeting trends, aesthetic judgment to fanciful taste, cultivation to social control, and expertise to social status. The two nineteenth-century inventions – the museum and the department store – seem equally fetishistic and depraved. Yet they also share a certain exquisiteness, created through the fineness of Couwenberg's handwork.

Apart from serving as metaphors for fine art, Couwenberg's stitched abstractions have an important place in her later work. With their geometric shapes, earth tones, and dark outlines, they bear a resemblance to analytic cubism, while their grid-like regularity gives them a topographical feel. Like all of Couwenberg's forms, they incite curiosity, perhaps even awe. Her working process for these pieces is very different from her three-dimensional works. Unlike her dress works, which demand that she perfectly execute a previously conceived pattern, she approaches these patterns, as she puts it "as a point of departure, something to reinterpret." As opposed to the architecture-like process of making the dresses, these pieces allow for improvisation and accident.

The stitched abstractions share an affinity with the work of Dada artist Hannah Höch, who incorporated dressmaking patterns into her collages beginning in the 1920s. In works such as *Design for the Memorial to an Important Lace Shirt* (1922), or *Tailor's Flower* (1920), Höch used bits of dressmaking and embroidery patterns as an abstract vocabulary of form. Like Couwenberg, she sought to invert aesthetic hierarchies subordinating design and textiles to high art practices and genres through the use of non-traditional media and techniques such as sewing. Couwenberg also shares with Höch a conceptualization of the dressmaking pattern as a form of abstraction germane to women's experience and specific to their own contexts as artists with backgrounds in design, fiber and craft.

Public Apparel/ Private Structures
(detail)
1995
pleated silk, reed, wire,
copper screen, cables
9 x 5 x 11in (23 x 13 x 29cm)

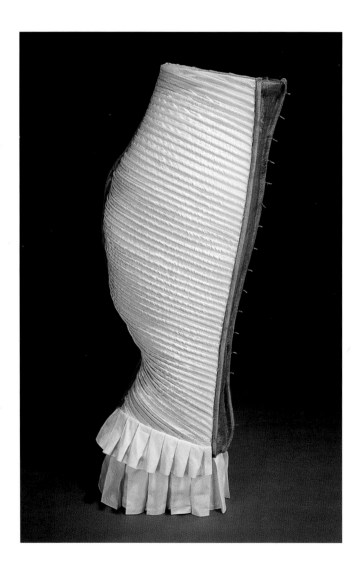

Untitled #4

1996

pleated silk, reed, feathers, wood,

copper screen

30 x 20 x 12in (78 x 52 x 31cm)

Individual Identity and Group Affiliation

Couwenberg's transition from the dress works to the series of wall works that followed is marked by *Untitled #4*, a piece from 1996 consisting of a bodice mounted to a wooden support that resembles the anchor of a wall sconce. Instead of supporting candles, the bodice holds protruding, breast-like, feathered mounds. Here the architectural connection is present, a sconce being an architectural fixture, but tangential. No longer autonomously supported, with the bodice abstracted from the body, this piece becomes a trophy. Bearing a resemblance to an animal's head mounted on a plaque, this work appears to be a biting commentary, intentional or not, on the objectification of women's bodies.

The trophy-like quality of the wall mounted bodice work prefigures Couwenberg's major series, *Family Air,* completed two years later. The unique wooden frames conceived for these works resemble heraldic shields. Within these frames, Couwenberg juxtaposes under small, glass domes small passages of crochet or bobbin lace and downy brown feathers against a stitched abstract ground.

The convex glass hermetically sealing these materials is in turn encased by the curiously shaped, broad, shield-like frames. In the case of at least one of the works in the series, *Family Air, AC* (1998), the shape of the frame is derived from the form produced by the corset upon the female body.

This series commemorates the women of Couwenberg's immediate family, hence its iconography carries specific references to their lives. The doilies, a collection that belonged to her grandmother, reference both her Dutch heritage and the weekly sewing circle held by Couwenberg's grandmother, mother, and aunts. Couwenberg's use of crochet and lace in these objects to represent women's traditional artistic practices and everyday domestic work, places them squarely within the larger feminist project involving the recovery of women's artistic heritage and the critique of the hierarchy of art and craft.

Couwenberg's *Family Air* series manifests new heights of ambiguity and strangeness. A shield-like frame suggest both a trophy and a sign of family lineage. Though their likenesses can be found throughout the United States, Couwenberg seems to draw upon their roots in the hoary families of Europe. In her hands, they combine nobility, evidenced by the heraldic form, with an atavistic ritualism, suggested by the tufts of fur-like feathers. They seem to belong to the Europe of the Saxons and the Huns, not the Germans and the French, of Norse mythology, not Romeo and Juliet. The simple, unembellished frames suggest a medieval coarseness and the central element, combining lace with feathers on an earthy ground, suggests a time when domestic life had not yet isolated itself from the realm of war and survival. It calls to mind a Europe when gallantry could not be distinguished from tribalism. It is an emblem of the continued existences of a clan, marking not greatness but steadfastness.

right:
Family Air #6
1998
flocked frame, seminole patchwork, dressmaking patterns, lace, feathers, computer embroidery, convex glass
51 x 90 x 1in
(133 x 234 x 2.6cm)

page 26:
Family Air #8
2000
overall dimensions:
27 x 38 x 1in
(70 x 99 x 2.6cm)

page 27:
Family Air #8 (detail)
flocked frame, digitized embroidery, dressmaking patterns, needle, thread, convex glass
14 x 17 x 1in
(36 x 44 x 2.6cm)

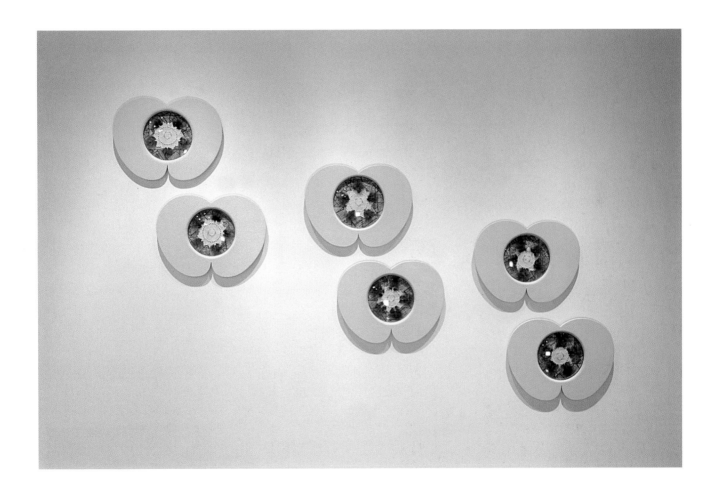

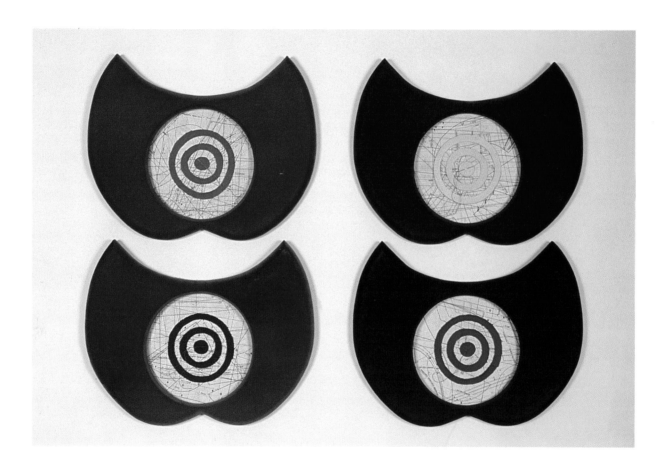

Two series of works initiated in 2000, the four wall-mounted collars and the *Embroidery Frolics,* lead up to Couwenberg's most recent series of digitized embroidery. The forms of the wall-mounted collars are derived from distinctive periods in costume history which the artist has reduced to essential, nearly abstract shapes and then blown-up to the gargantuan size of seven feet in width. Oversize, steel T-pins 'hold down' the collars like that of the splayed body undergoing autopsy or dissection.

The *Embroidery Frolics* share a certain resemblance to the *Family Air* series through the use of flocked, wooden frames that encase collage elements. In this series, several transparent layers of printed and machine embroidered fabrics are secured with dress-making pins in the manner of insect specimens mounted in shadowboxes. Two images dominate the *Embroidery Frolic:* the target and one of several basic dress forms

repeated across the visual field. Although the target is the ground for the transparent layer of embroidered dress forms, the two images actually compete for the viewer's attention and they cannot be focused upon simultaneously. In the series *Precious View* (2002), the private references to family keepsakes through the shape of the flocked frames is combined with references to the very public world of naval rank and insignia. This work foregrounds what is present among both series, the tension between one's desire for group identity, the conformity it requires, and the quest for personal distinction.

Underlying Couwenberg's shields, dress-works, collars, and framed embroideries is a profound humanism. In Thomas Carlyle's 1833 book, *'Sartor Resartus'* [The Tailor Retailored], we find a line that seems to serve as the enigmatic key to all of Couwenberg's mysterious forms: "all Emblematic things are properly Clothes."

An emblem is a sign of belonging to a social body. To posses an emblem introduces, then, a paradox of belonging: that distinctions conferred on the individual cannot be solely individual but must also be properties of a group. This is the reason that all emblems are clothes. Though clothes are worn by individuals, they necessarily signify the group. Couwenberg's Victorian bustle is only an extreme case of what is always true and what comes to light in her shields, that clothing is a sign and like all signs it only functions within a greater system wherein that sign is given meaning. All clothes, like all emblems, are tribal.

In '*Sartor Resartus*,' we also find the line: "The beginning of all Wisdom is to look fixedly on Clothes... till they become transparent." Looking at any one of Couwenberg's works gives a sense of being in the proximity of wisdom. Viewers are asked to look at clothes in order to see sociability.

All her works remind us that clothes, like houses, mark the boundary between private and public and so belong essentially to both realms. The inextricable connection in her work between body and dress only reminds us that bodies are always, in a sense, clothed. She reminds us that we never stand naked in the world because our bodies are continually defined and coded by society, even as we participate in the process. This is what Gilles Deleuze and Félix Guattari mean when they say "you will articulate your body." In Couwenberg's work, the essential affinity between body and clothes relates to her insistence that the sea is defined by the shore. Thereby clothes are a metaphor for meaning itself whereby our attempt to make meaning out of the world always depends on our willingness to tailor the forms of meaning (the patterns, if you will) that are already given to us.

Ellissa Auther & **Adam Lerner**

above:
Dutch Ruffled Collar
2001
3-D Studio Max computer rendering

Color Plates

left:
**Seeing is Forgetting
the Thing One Sees**
1987
copper screen, reed, wood,
cable, weight
55 x 20 x 24in (143 x 52 x 62cm)

pages 32 & 33
Embroidery Frolic #1 & #2
2000
digitized embroidery, fabric, pins,
flock, shadowbox
21 x 17 x 1.5in (55 x 44 x 4cm)

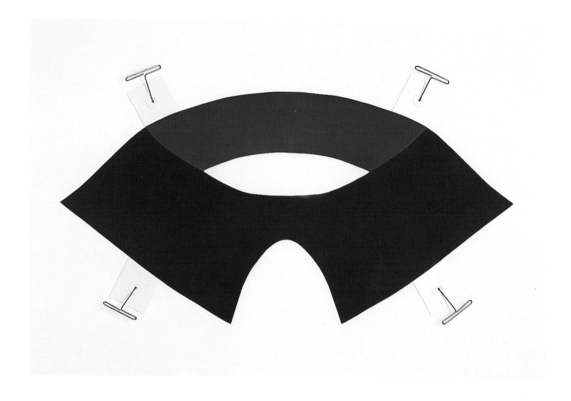

Flat Collar #2
2000
flock, masonite, steel T-pins
42 x 84in (109 x 216cm)
T-pins 11 x 7in (29 x 18cm)

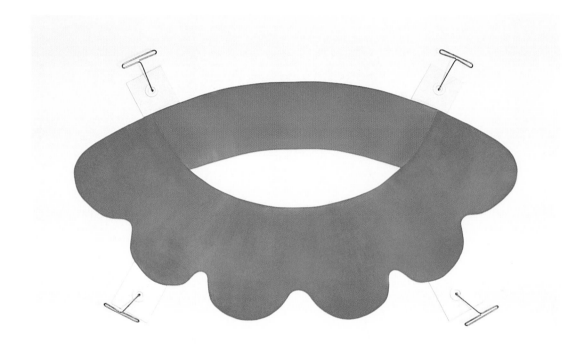

Flat Collar #1
2000
flock, masonite, steel T-pins
42 x 84in (109 x 216cm)
T pins: 11 x 7in (29 x 18cm)

this page and opposite:
Das Boat
Annet Couwenberg & Kathleen O'Meara
2001
hand-constructed Aleutian Bidarka Kayak,
wood, canvas, flax, polyurethane

pages 40, 41:
The Legs, Arms and Stomach
2001 (details)
digitized embroidery, flock,
dressmaking patterns, shadowbox
15 x 12 x 11.5in (39 x 31 x 30cm)

page 38:
Family Air #4 1998
seminole patchwork, dressmaking
patterns, lace, feathers, convex glass
27 x 21 x 2in (70 x 55 x 5cm)

page 39:
Family Air #6 (detail) 1998
flocked frame, seminole patchwork,
dressmaking patterns, lace,feathers,
computer embroidery, convex glass
14 x 18 x 1in (36 x 47 x 2.6cm)

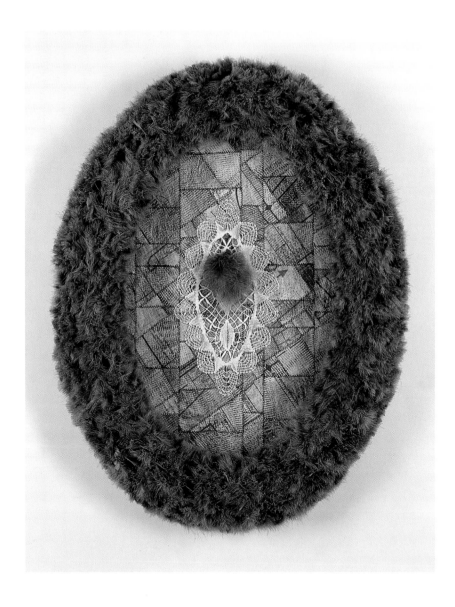

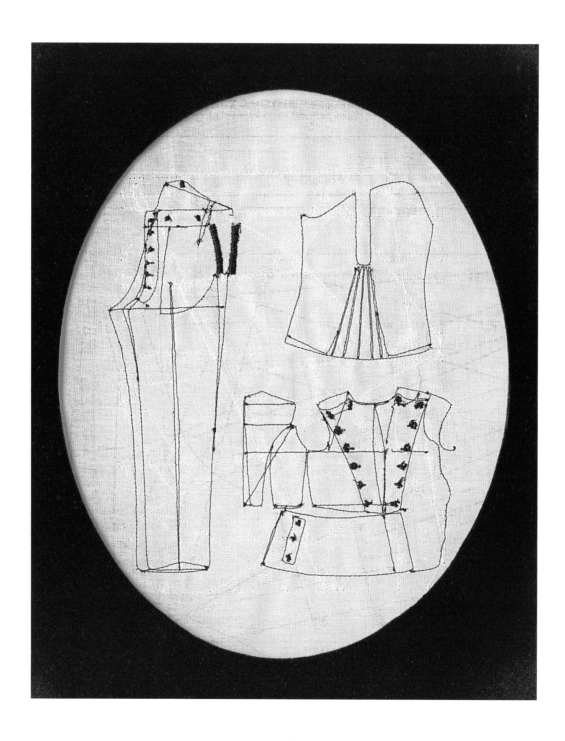

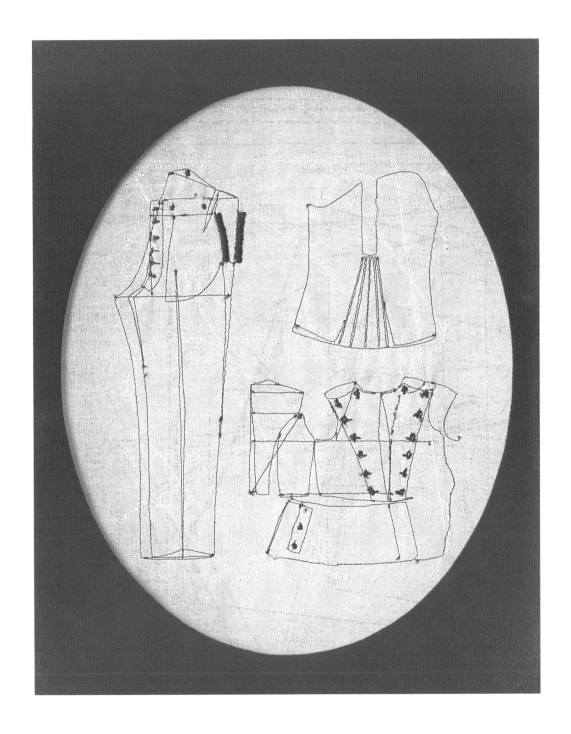

above:

Callous Collar

1996

coiled copper wire,

reed, aluminium wire

24 x 24 x 6in (62 x 62 x 16cm)

right:

Act Normal and That's Crazy Enough

2002

starched cotton, reed, copper wire, computer

embroidery, fabric

19 x 112 x 140in (49 x 291 x 364cm)

Biography

Born

1950	Rotterdam, The Netherlands

Education and Awards

1974	B.F.A in Textile Arts and Educational Degree, School for Textiles, De Windroos, Rotterdam, The Netherlands
1983	M.F.A., Textile Arts, Syracuse University, Syracuse, NY
1986	M.F.A., Cranbrook Academy of Art, Bloomfield Hills, MI
1988	Murphy Education Grant
1989	Ohio Arts Council Individual Artist Award
1997, 2000, 2003	Maryland State Arts Council Individual Artist Award

Professional

1989 to present	Chair, Fiber Department, Maryland Institute College of Art, Baltimore, MD

Selected Solo Exhibitions

2004	'Annet Couwenberg,' Delaware Center for Contemporary Arts, Wilmington, DE
2003	'Annet Couwenberg and Piper Shepard,' 28th Street Studio, New York, NY
2000	'Re-addressing Fiber,' Park School Gallery, Brooklandville, MD
1999	'Wearing Down Thin, Reconfigurations by Annet Couwenberg,' Recitation Hall Gallery, Newark, Delaware
1996	'Under Construction: The work of Annet Couwenberg,' City Gallery, Atlanta, GA
1995	'Annet Couwenberg and David Page: Recent Work,' Maryland Art Place, Baltimore, MD (two person show)
1994	'Public Apparel/Private Structures,' Gormley Gallery, College of Notre Dame, Baltimore, MD
1988	'Signalement,' Nederlands Textielmuseum, Tilburg, The Netherlands

Selected Group Exhibitions

2003	'Wrestling,' Rosenberg Gallery, Goucher College, Baltimore, MD
	'Common Thread,' Tobey Gallery, Memphis, TN
2002	'Bizarre Beeldenbos', Nederlands Textielmuseum, Tilburg, The Netherlands
	'Les Fables de la Fontaine', Centre pour l'Art et la Culture, Aix-en Provence, France (tour Italy and USA)
2001	'Invented Objects, Imagined Spaces,' Maryland Art Place, Baltimore, MD
2000	'Snapshot,' Contemporary Museum, Baltimore, MD
	'Trunk Show,' Zoller Gallery, University Park, Pennsylvania (tour)
1999	'Embodiment,' The Arkansas Arts Center, Little Rock, AR
1997	'A Permeable Edge: Reference Body/Figure,' Emerson Gallery, McLean, VA (tour)
	'Transformation: Fiber Orientation,' Dowd Fine Arts Gallery, Cortland, NY
	'Hidden Realities, Secret Visions,' Pascal Center for Performing Arts Gallery, Arnold, MD
1995	'Material Poetry,' Katherine Nash Gallery, Minneapolis, MN
1992	'Natural Forces/ Human Observations,' The Kemper Gallery, The Kansas City Art Institute, MO
1991	'De Verzameling in Beeld,' Textielmuseum, Tilburg, The Netherlands
1990	'Design in Sculptural Fiber,' Craft Alliance Gallery, St. Louis, MO
1989	'Contemporary Fibers,' Moreau Gallery, St. Mary's College, Notre Dame, IN
1987	'Kent-Blossom/ Art' School of Art Gallery, Kent State University, OH
1986	Juried group show, The Detroit Institute of Art, Detroit, MI
1985	'Constructions,' Detroit Focus Gallery, Detroit, MI
1982	Resort Show, Fashion Designer Ronald Kolodzie,Brooke Alexander Gallery, New York, NY
	Julie Artisans Gallery, New York, NY
1981	Spring Show, Fashion Designer Ronald Kolodzie, New York, NY

Selected Bibliography

2002	*La Provence*, April 13, 'Ces Gens de la Fontaine,' by Samir Hedder
	Aix en Dialogue, March 22, 'Les Fables de la Fontaine', by Jean Francois
2001	*Surface Design Journal* Vol 26, No 1, 'Feminism and Fiber: A History of Art Criticism,' essay by Jean Robertson
	'Obsession' (brochure), Rosenberg Gallery, Goucher College, Baltimore, essay by Laura Burns
2000	*Surface Design Journal,* Vol 25, No 1, Annet Couwenberg: 'Emblems of Containment,' essay by Susan Isaacs (pp29-35)
	'Re-addressing fiber: New works by Annet Couwenberg' (brochure), Park School Gallery, Brooklandville, essay by Peter Bruun
1999	*Sculpture*, October, Annet Couwenberg, review by Jan Gardner Broske
	Fiberarts, Sept/Oct, Wearing Down Thin; Reconfigurations by Annet Couwenberg, essay by Jan Gardner Broske (p58)
	'Embodiment' (catalog), The Arkansas Arts Center Decorative Arts Museum, essay by Alan Du Bois
	The Review, February 12 'Dutch woman's art exhibit glows at UD's Recitation Hall Gallery,' review by Kevin Etienne-Cummings
	'Wearing Down Thin, Reconfigurations by Annet Couwenberg ' (catalog), essay by J.Susan Isaacs
1998	*Fiberarts*, Summer, 'A Permeable Edge' by Laura McGough
	Sculpture, Jan 1998, 'A Permeable Edge: Reference body/figure,' by George Howell

Selected Bibliography continued

1997	*The Dragon Chronicle*, Nov. 4, 'Women's Art Show at Dowd,' review by Phillip Hendrickson
	Syracuse Herald American, Nov. 30, review by Sherry Chayat
	<NO> (Nouvel Object) III, Seoul, South Korea, essay by Warren Seelig
	'A Permeable Edge: Reference body/figure' (catalog), essay by Dr. Linda McGreevy
1996	*Fiberarts*, Sept/Oct, Annet Couwenberg: Under Construction, review by Donald D Keyes,
	Under Construction: The Work of Annet Couwenberg (catalog), essay by Nicholas Corrin
	The Atlanta Constitution, April 26, 1996, 'Hemstitching as a Route to Freedom,'
	review by Pamela Blume-Leonard
1995	*Fiberarts*, Summer, 'Shifting Perception,' essay by William Easton
	City Paper, April 19, 'Of Human Bondage,' review by Mike Giuliano, Baltimore, MD
	The Baltimore Sun, April 5, 'Restraints Provide a Compelling Theme at MAP,'
	review by John Dorsey
1994	*Fiberarts*, Summer, 'A Plea For Broader Dialogue,' essay by Anne Wilson
1992	*The Kansas City Star*, February 9, Modern Concerns Inspire Dramatic Modern Sculpture,
	review by Alice Thorson
	Pitch, February 9, 'Technology and Nature: A Juxtaposition of Forces,'
	review by Deane Pearson, Kansas, MO
1989	*Natural Forces/ Human Observations* (catalog), essay by Margo Mensing
	Southbend Tribune, November 12, 'Cutting Edge,' review by Jeanne Derbeck, IN
	Sun Scoop Journal, May 4, by Dave Rowe, Cleveland, OH

Media

1994	Radio Interview, WJHU with Lisa Simone, Baltimore, MD

Public Collection

Nederlands Textielmusem, Tilburg, The Netherlands

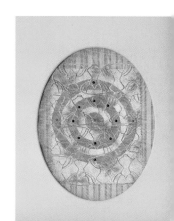